Turkey Travel Guide 2023

Elizabeth allen

```
Table of Contents
```

Introduction

Overview of Turkey
History and Culture
Geography and Climate

Planning Your Trip

Best Time to Visit
Entry Requirements and Visa Information
Health and Safety Tips
Transportation Options
Currency and Money Matters
Language and Communication

```
Istanbul
```

Overview of Istanbul
 Top Attractions
 Historical Sites
Museums and Galleries
Shopping and Markets
Dining and Cuisine

Nightlife and Entertainment
Day Trips from Istanbul

Cappadocia

Overview of Cappadocia
Fairy Chimneys and Unique Landscapes
Hot Air Balloon Rides
Underground Cities and Cave Dwellings
Hiking and Outdoor Activities
Local Cuisine and Wine Tasting Accommodation Options

Turkey's Overview

Turkey, officially known as the Republic of Turkey, is a crosscountry tracked down generally on the Anatolian Expanse of land in Western Asia, with a more unobtrusive piece on the Balkan Projection in Southeast Europe. Lined by eight countries and incorporated by three particular seas, Turkey stands firm on a noteworthy geographical balance interfacing Europe and Asia. Its different social heritage, rich history, stunning scenes, and exuberant metropolitan networks make it a hypnotizing objective for explorers and a gigantic player in the locale.

Geographically, Turkey wraps a wide variety of scenes, including colossal mountain ranges, productive valleys, wonderful coastlines, and broad levels. The country is home to the Pontic Mountains in the north, the Taurus

Mountains in the south, and the Anatolian Level, which controls the central district. Turkey is similarly known for the Bosporus and Dardanelles streams, which interface the Dull Sea to the Mediterranean and separate Europe from Asia.

Turkey has a general population of more than 82 million people, making it maybe of the most long distance country on earth. The majority of the general population is of Turkish personality and practices Islam as the otherworldly religion, yet the country is known for its severe and ethnic assortment. Turkish is the power language, and Istanbul, the greatest city, fills in as the monetary, social, and legitimate point of convergence of the country.

Overall, Turkey has been a help of progress, with a legacy that crosses centuries. It was the beginning of the Byzantine Domain and the Ottoman Space, the two of which left a persevering through impact on the district to say the very least. Hence, Turkey is touched with evident regions and out of date ruins, for instance, the remarkable Hagia Sophia and Topkapi Imperial home in Istanbul, the old city of Ephesus, and the stone game plans of Cappadocia.

Despite its evident and social heritage, Turkey offers an alternate extent of attractions. The country has a thriving the movement business, attracting visitors with its great coastlines along the Aegean and Mediterranean coasts, as Bodrum, Antalya, and Fethiye. Outside aficionados can explore the stunning scenes of Pamukkale, Mount Ararat, and the pixie smokestack piles of Cappadocia. Turkey is furthermore known for its luscious cooking, blending Center Eastern, Central Asian, and Mediterranean effects.

Decisively, Turkey is a parliamentary republic with a mixed economy and an alternate present day region. It has been a person from NATO starting around 1952 and has searched for closer joins with the European Affiliation, yet the increment cycle has gone up against various challenges. Turkey expects a basic part in neighborhood official issues, particularly practically identical to the persistent battles in the Middle East, and is a key travel point for exiles and homeless people searching for section into Europe.

In any case, it is crucial for observe that Turkey has defied political and social troubles lately. Issues like political polarization, the option to talk openly of talk, and fundamental freedoms have been subjects of local and overall concern. These troubles an influence the country's standing and relationship with a part of its overall assistants.

In summation, Turkey is a country with a rich social heritage, stunning scenes, and a fundamental region at the intersection of Europe and Asia. From its undeniable achievements to its generally expected greatness, Turkey offers a blend of old practices and current experiences, making it an enchanting goal for explorers and a huge player in the region.

Turkey's History & Culture

Turkey, officially known as the Republic of Turkey, is a crosscountry tracked down generally on the Anatolian Projection in Western Asia, with a more unobtrusive piece on the Balkan Body of land in Southeast Europe. It has a rich and different history and culture that navigates centuries, blending influences from various civic establishments and domains that have formed the region. Here is a diagram of the arrangement of encounters and culture of Turkey.

History:

Old Metro foundations: The locale that is as of now Turkey has been had since antiquated times. It was home to different old metro foundations, including the Hittites, Phrygians, Lydians, and Persians. The area later went under the effect of the Greek city-states and over the long haul tumbled to Alexander the Exceptional.

Byzantine Domain: With the rot of the Roman Space, the eastern part, known as the Byzantine Domain, emerged, with its capital at Constantinople (as of now Istanbul). The Byzantines safeguarded and encouraged the Greco-Roman culture and expected a gigantic part in the spread of Christianity.

Ottoman Domain: In the thirteenth 100 years, the Seljuk Turks appeared in Anatolia and consistently settled control over the area. They were thusly won by the Ottoman Turks, who expanded their domain, showing up at its top in the sixteenth and seventeenth many years. The Ottoman Space integrated bits of Southeast Europe,

Western Asia, and North Africa. Istanbul transformed into the capital and a point of convergence of Islamic advancement.

Present day Turkey: The ruin of the Ottoman Domain arranged for the groundwork of the Republic of Turkey in 1923, under the organization of Mustafa Kemal Atatürk. Atatürk began a movement of changes highlighted modernizing the country and transforming it into a standard and vote based country.

Culture:

Religion: the majority of the general population in Turkey is Muslim, with Islam being the dominating religion. Regardless, Turkey has a typical government, and chance of religion is guaranteed by the constitution. The country has an alternate severe scene, with basic Christian and Jewish social class as well.

Language: The power language of Turkey is Turkish, which has a spot with the Turkic language family. Turkish is spoken by a large portion of the general population, yet various vernaculars, similar to Kurdish, Arabic, and Armenian, are furthermore spoken by minority social occasions.

Cooking: Turkish food is popular for its rich flavors and variety. It is a blend of Central Asian, Center Eastern, Mediterranean, and Balkan cooking styles. Notable dishes consolidate kebabs, baklava, Turkish tea, Turkish coffee, and meze (a decision of little dishes filled in as canapés).

Articulations and Plan: Turkish articulations and designing have been affected by various human progressions since the dawn of time. Noteworthy models recall the Hagia Sophia and the Blue Mosque for Istanbul, as well as the stone cut sanctuaries of Cappadocia. Turkish carpets, pottery creation, calligraphy, and more modest than normal materials are similarly uncommonly regarded kinds of workmanship.

Customs and Festivities: Turkey has a rich weaving of customs and festivities that are lauded all through the country. A part of the tremendous festivals consolidate Eid al-Fitr (the completion of Ramadan), Republic Day (recollecting the groundwork of the republic), and Mevlana Festivity (regarding the thirteenth century Sufi essayist Rumi).

Music and Dance: Turkish music has an alternate extent of types, including old style Ottoman music, individuals music, and current Turkish well known music. Ordinary Turkish instruments, for instance, the oud, saz, and ney are by and large used. Individuals moves like the Horon, Halay, and Zeybek are renowned kinds of customary dance.

This layout gives a short investigate the enormous history and vivacious culture of Turkey. In any case, it is vital for observe that Turkey's arrangement of encounters and culture are convoluted and complex, with nearby.

Topography and Climate of Turkey

Turkey is a crosscountry tracked down generally on the Anatolian Body of land in Western Asia, with a more unassuming piece on the Balkan Projection in Southeast Europe. Its clever land position makes Turkey an expansion among Europe and Asia, connecting the Mediterranean Sea to the Dim Sea. We ought to dive into the geography and climate of Turkey.

Geography:
Turkey has an alternate scene that consolidates mountains, levels, coastline fields, and stream valleys. The country is lined by eight countries: Greece and Bulgaria toward the northwest, Georgia toward the upper east, Armenia, Azerbaijan, and Iran eastward, and Iraq and Syria southward. Its shore expands in excess of 7,200 kilometers (4,500 miles), lined by the Aegean Sea westward, the Mediterranean Sea southward, and the Dull Sea northward.

The central district of Turkey is overpowered by the Anatolian Level, an enormous raised locale containing high fields and moving slants. The country's most critical zenith, Mount Ararat, shows up at an ascent of 5,137 meters (16,854 feet) and is arranged in the eastern piece of the country. The Taurus Mountains connect along the southern coast, giving a stunning setting and having a prominent effect between the Mediterranean climate along the coast and the central area climate inland.

Turkey is moreover home to a couple of basic streams, including the Euphrates, Tigris, and the longest stream a totally inside Turkish region, the Kızılırmak. These streams give water resources for cultivation and hydroelectric power age.

Climate:
Turkey experiences an alternate extent of conditions due to its tremendous geographical degree. The climate changes from Mediterranean along the waterfront locales

to central area in within, with sloping regions having their own microclimates. Here are the very climatic locale:

Mediterranean Climate: The shoreline regions of Turkey, including the Aegean and Mediterranean coasts, have a Mediterranean climate depicted by boiling, dry summers and delicate, wet winters. Summers are regularly boiling and dry, with temperatures outperforming 30°C (86°F), while winters are delicate and get most of the yearly precipitation.

Central area Climate: Inland Anatolia has a central area climate with rankling, dry summers and cold, freezing winters. Temperatures can reach 40°C (104°F) in summer, while winter temperatures as often as possible diminishing underneath freezing, with basic snowfall in the rough regions.

Dim Sea Climate: The northern ocean front locales along the Dim Sea have a quiet climate influenced by the sea. Summers are warm and tacky, while winters are delicate and wet. This locale gets ample precipitation reliably.

Eastern Anatolia Climate: The eastern piece of Turkey, including the undeniable levels and mountain ranges, experiences a more ruthless climate. Winters are freezing, with significant snowfall, and summers are short and cool.

Southeastern Anatolia Climate: This locale has a semi-completely dry to dry climate with warm summers and delicate winters. It is depicted by low precipitation and high temperatures, particularly all through the mid year months.

These assortments in climate add to the rich biodiversity of Turkey, making it a characteristic environmental factors for various vegetation.

In frame, Turkey's geography goes from mountains and levels to shoreline fields, while its current circumstance shifts from Mediterranean along the coast to central area and dried in within. This assortment in geography and climate adds to the country's customary greatness and supports countless organic frameworks.

Orchestrating your visit

Best Time for Turkey Visit

The best an open door to visit Turkey by and large depends upon the specific region you mean to research and the activities you have as an essential concern. Turkey has an alternate climate as a result of its enormous land and topographical assortments. Here is a breakdown of the best times to visit different bits of Turkey:

Istanbul and the Marmara Region: The best an open door to visit Istanbul and the Marmara District is during spring (April to May) and collect time (September to October). The weather patterns is delicate, and the city is less pressed appeared differently in relation to the pre-summer months. Spring brings growing blooms and magnificent temperatures, while pre-winter offers a brilliant exhibit of assortments.

Aegean and Mediterranean Floats: The best an open door to visit the ocean front areas of Turkey, including notable protests like Bodrum, Antalya, and Fethiye, is all through the pre-summer months (June to August). The atmospheric conditions is boiling and splendid, allowing you to participate in the wonderful coastlines and completely clear waters. In any case, recall that this is furthermore the apex explorer season, so expect greater gatherings.

Cappadocia and Central Anatolia: Cappadocia, known for its fascinating stone courses of action and traveler expand rides, is best visited during spring and pre-winter. The environment during these seasons is moderate, making it ideal for outside activities and examination. The touring inflatable season usually starts in Spring and runs until November.

Eastern Anatolia and Dim Sea Region: Accepting you expect to visit Eastern Anatolia or the Dull Sea Locale, the pre-summer months (June to September) are the most sensible. These locales experience colder winters and a more restricted summer season. Summer offers awesome temperatures and superb scenes, including rich vegetation and stunning lakes.

Winter Sports in Eastern Turkey: If you're enthused about winter sports like skiing and snowboarding, the most obvious opportunity to visit Turkey's ski resorts in the eastern piece of the nation, as Palandöken and Uludağ, is all through the chilly climate months (December to February).

Visa Prohibitions:

Inhabitants of explicit countries are rejected from getting a visa and can enter Turkey for the movement business or business purposes for a confined term. These exemptions change dependent upon the country of citizenship and the length of stay permitted. A couple of cases of visa-barred countries integrate the US, the Bound together Domain, Canada, Australia, and various European Endorser states. The term of stay regularly goes from 30 to 90 days inside a 180-day period of time. Nevertheless, the

particular nuances can differentiate, so checking the continuous rules for your specific nation is huge.
e-Visa:

Most explorers who require a visa to enter Turkey can get an e-Visa, an electronic visa that can be applied for online preceding traveling. The e-Visa is a direct and supportive strategy for getting a visa, discarding the need to visit a Turkish worldwide place of refuge or division. The application cycle ordinarily requires wrapping up an online construction, making the fundamental portions, and getting the e-Visa through email. The e-Visa is generally significant for the movement business and business purposes and allows stays of up to 90 days inside a 180-day time period. The cost and unequivocal requirements could change, so it's principal to insinuate the power e-Visa site for exact and present day information.
Visa on Appearance:

A couple of personalities that are not equipped for an e-Visa can regardless get a visa on arriving in Turkish air terminals. Regardless, it's imperative to observe that the availability of visa on appearance could change, and it is all around recommended to gain an e-Visa before going out to avoid any potential issues.

Work and Home Awards:

If you expect to work or stay in Turkey for an extensive period, you will presumably need to get a work award or a home permit. Work awards are consistently gained by organizations for their delegates, while home licenses are normal for individuals who wish to stay in Turkey due to reasons like work, tutoring, or family reunification. The application cycle for work and home awards can be confounding and may require supporting reports, so it's fitting to converse with the huge subject matter experts or your supervisor for positive information.

Yet again assuming no one minds, note that visa rules can change, so checking the continuous essentials and methodologies with the power Turkish subject matter experts or the nearest Turkish worldwide place of refuge or office preceding making any development arrangements is huge.

Turkey Visit Security Tips

While visiting Turkey, it's crucial to zero in on your prosperity and security to ensure an exquisite and easy experience. The following are a couple of key tips to recollect:

Stay hydrated: Turkey's current circumstance can be boiling and dry, especially all through the mid year months. Convey a water bottle with you reliably and drink a ton of fluids to avoid drying out.

Practice safe food and water tidiness: Be careful about the food and water you finish. Stick to bundled or percolated water, and make an effort not to drink unrefined or half-cooked meats and fish. Pick recently ready and hot meals from genuine establishments.

Tidy up a significant part of the time: Real hand neatness is key to prevent the spread of organisms and disorders. Tidy up with cleaning agent and water for somewhere near 20 seconds preceding eating, right after using the washroom, and resulting to reaching surfaces in open areas.

Safeguard yourself from the sun: Turkey's abundant light can be serious, so shield yourself from sun related consume and heatstroke. Wear sunscreen with a high SPF, use a cap, shades, and lightweight, breathable dress to safeguard yourself from the sun's perilous pillars.

Be careful about street food: Turkish street food is luscious and a gigantic piece of the close by experience. In any case, pick dealers adroitly. Look for places with high client turnover and clean food status locales. Ensure that the food is arranged totally and served hot.

Stay revived on vaccinations: Before going out to Turkey, talk with your clinical benefits provider to ensure that you are remarkable on routine inoculations. Dependent upon your schedule things and clinical history, additional inoculations may be proposed.

Avoid any and all risks against bugs: In unambiguous areas of Turkey, bugs like mosquitoes can be unavoidable, especially during summer. Use bug repellent, wear long-sleeved dress, and think about leftover in offices with screens or cooling to restrict receptiveness.

Practice safe transportation: If you expect to rent a vehicle or using public transportation, center around security. Comply with traffic rules, wear seat straps reliably, and make an effort not to drive during top hours in stopped up districts. Use good transportation benefits and watch out for your own resources.

Stay informed about neighborhood customs and rules: Get to know close by guidelines, customs, and social norms to avoid accidentally bringing offense or getting into difficulty. Respect severe objections, dress honestly when fundamental, and know about area responsive characteristics.

Secure your resources: Like in any voyager objective, watch out for your own belongings. Use secure packs or rucksacks, keep your resources hidden away, and make an effort not to show huge amount of cash or expensive pearls without any attempt at being subtle.

Remember, these tips are generally rules, and it's constantly truly brilliant to investigate unequivocal prosperity and security ideas for the particular regions you mean to visit in Turkey. Stay vigilant, practice great judgment, and have an extraordinary and safe trip!

Transportation Decisions in Turkey

Client
Form on transportation decisions in turkey

ChatGPT
Turkey offers an alternate extent of transportation decisions for both local and worldwide pioneers. From current air terminals and especially related streets to a wide rail course association and a collection of public transportation structures, getting around the country is

to some degree basic. The following are a piece of the transportation decisions open in Turkey:

Air Travel: Turkey has different air terminals, with Istanbul Ataturk Air terminal and Istanbul Sabiha Gokcen Air terminal being the most dynamic. These air terminals go about as huge habitats for both local and worldwide flights. Turkish Airplanes, the public carrier, offers wide local and worldwide courses, communicating critical metropolitan regions inside Turkey and various protests all around the planet. There are furthermore a couple of neighborhood air terminals serving notable traveler areas like Antalya, Izmir, and Bodrum.

Intercity Transports: Turkey has a high level intercity transport association, which is one of the most renowned strategies for transportation for the two neighborhood individuals and travelers. Associations like Metro Turizm, Ulusoy, and Kamil Koç work standard vehicle organizations communicating metropolitan regions and towns generally through the country. The vehicles are pleasant, cooled, and offer various comforts, settling on them a supportive and sensible decision for development.

Trains: Turkey has an expansive rail line network worked by the Turkish State Rail courses (TCDD). The rail course system interfaces critical metropolitan networks like Istanbul, Ankara, Izmir, and Adana, as well as additional humble towns and areas. Fast trains, for instance, the Ankara-Istanbul and Ankara-Konya courses, give a speedy and useful strategy for going between metropolitan networks. The trains offer different classes, including economy and business, with open to seating and locally accessible workplaces.

Metro and Streetcars: Critical metropolitan regions in Turkey, including Istanbul, Ankara, and Izmir, have progressed metro and trolley structures. Istanbul, explicitly, has an expansive metro network that covers various bits of the city. These structures offer a supportive strategy for going inside the metropolitan districts, avoiding gridlock and giving rapid permission to popular attractions, business region, and neighborhoods.

Taxis: Cabs are extensively open in Turkey's metropolitan networks and towns. They can be hailed in the city or found at allocated taxi stands. In greater metropolitan regions like Istanbul and Ankara, taxi organizations could offer both standard taxis and ride-waving to decisions through compact applications. Taxis in Turkey are overall metered, yet it is fitting to ensure the meter is running or choose an expense preceding starting the outing.

Dolmuş: Dolmuş is a typical minibus or van organization for the most part used for transportation inside metropolitan networks and towns, too concerning short intercity trips. They work on fixed courses and pick and drop off voyagers in transit. Dolmuş vehicles are by and large assortment coded and have express stops, making them a keen and supportive strategy for transportation, especially for additional restricted distances.

Ships and Boats: Turkey's waterfront regions, including the Aegean and Mediterranean coasts, offer boat helps that interface various islands, shoreline towns, and metropolitan networks. Istanbul moreover has standard boat organizations working across the Bosporus Stream, communicating the European and Asian sides of the city. These boats are utilitarian transportation decisions as well as give lovely points of view and enchanting experiences.

While going inside Turkey, key to think about the transportation decision best suits your necessities, goal, and spending plan. It's critical that during top travel seasons, for instance, events and mid year months, it's judicious to book transportation tickets early on to get your leaned toward technique for development and schedule.

Turkish Money and Cash.

Turkey has an alternate and dynamic economy, and its endlessly cash matters expect a critical part in framing its money related scene. Here is a blueprint of the money.

Money:

The authority money of Turkey is the Turkish lira (Attempt). The Turkish lira is indicated by the image "₺" and is partitioned into 100 kurus. Banknotes come in sections of 5, 10, 20, 50, 100, 200, and 500 lira, while coins are accessible in 1, 5, 10, 25, and 50 kurus, as well as 1 lira.

Trade Rates:
The conversion scale of the Turkish lira can vary because of different elements, including monetary circumstances, political solidness, and market influences. It is crucial for monitor trade rates in the event that you are wanting to change over monetary standards or participate in worldwide exchanges including the Turkish lira.

Expansion and Financial Strategy:
Expansion has been difficult for Turkey. High expansion rates can influence the buying influence of the cash and dissolve the worth of cash over the long haul. The National Bank of the Republic of Turkey (CBRT) assumes a pivotal part in planning and executing financial strategy to keep up with value steadiness and control expansion.

The CBRT utilizes different devices, for example, loan fees and save necessities, to deal with the cash supply and settle the economy.

Monetary Organizations:
Turkey has an advanced financial area containing public, private, and unfamiliar banks. These foundations give a scope of monetary administrations, including store accounts, credits, Mastercards, and speculation potential open doors. The financial area in Turkey is controlled by the Financial Guideline and Management Organization (BRSA) to guarantee soundness and safeguard the interests of contributors.

Electronic Installments and Advanced Banking:
Turkey has seen huge development in electronic installments and computerized financial administrations lately. Portable banking applications and online installment stages have become progressively famous, offering advantageous and secure choices for monetary exchanges. Also, credit and check card use is far reaching

in Turkey, with card installments acknowledged in many foundations.

Unfamiliar Trade Guidelines:
Turkey has explicit guidelines with respect to unfamiliar cash trade and exchanges. People and organizations should consent to these guidelines while changing over monetary forms, moving assets abroad, or participating in unfamiliar exchange. It is fitting to talk with approved banks or monetary foundations to guarantee consistence with appropriate guidelines.

The travel industry and Money Trade:
As a well known traveler objective, Turkey has various cash trade workplaces situated in vacationer regions and significant urban communities. It is critical to be mindful while trading cash and consider contrasting trade rates and charges with get the best arrangement.

By and large, cash and cash matters in Turkey include the utilization of Turkish lira, contemplations of trade rates, overseeing expansion, drawing in with monetary organizations, embracing computerized banking, and complying to unfamiliar trade guidelines. Staying up to date with monetary turns of events and looking for proficient exhortation can assist people and organizations with exploring the monetary scene in Turkey successfully

Turkey's Etymological Variety

Language and correspondence in Turkey are described by a rich and various semantic scene, formed by verifiable, social, and political elements. The authority language of Turkey is Turkish, which is spoken by most of the populace and fills in as the essential method for correspondence the nation over. In any case, Turkey is likewise home to different minority dialects and lingos.

Turkish is an individual from the Turkic language family and offers likenesses with other Turkic dialects spoken in Focal Asia and the Center East. It utilizes the Latin letter set, which was presented in 1928 as a feature of Kemal Atatürk's language change to supplant the recently utilized Arabic content. This change assumed a critical part in modernizing the Turkish language and making it more open.

Notwithstanding Turkish, a few minority dialects are spoken in Turkey. Kurdish, a language with its own particular lingos, is spoken by a critical piece of the populace, essentially in the southeastern districts of the country. Other minority dialects incorporate Arabic, Circassian, Laz, and Armenian, among others. These dialects are many times utilized inside their particular networks and social settings.

Correspondence in Turkey is affected by social standards and social orders. Turkish society puts significance on regard, courteousness, and customs, especially while connecting with elderly folks or those in, important, influential places. It is normal for individuals to involve honorifics and titles while tending to others as a noble gesture. For instance, utilizing "Bey" (Mr.) or "Hanim" (Mrs./Ms.) after somebody's name is a typical practice.

Motions and non-verbal communication likewise assume a part in correspondence in Turkey. Individuals frequently use hand motions, for example, pointing with the pointer or raising the thumb to communicate arrangement or endorsement. Eye to eye connection is by and large expected, as it is viewed as an indication of mindfulness and regard. In any case, it's vital to take note of that social standards and correspondence styles can shift across various locales and networks inside Turkey.

Lately, headways in innovation and the far and wide utilization of the web and virtual entertainment essentially affect correspondence designs in Turkey. Like in numerous different nations, virtual entertainment stages, informing applications, and online specialized devices have become progressively famous for remaining associated and sharing data.

In general, language and correspondence in Turkey mirror the country's different social legacy and the novel mix of authentic impacts. The Turkish language, with its own particular qualities and varieties, fills in as the essential method for correspondence, while minority dialects add to the phonetic variety of the country. Understanding and regarding these etymological and social subtleties are fundamental for successful correspondence in Turkey.

ISTANBUL

Istanbul Outline

Istanbul, generally known as Byzantium and Constantinople, is an energetic and enrapturing city that rides both Europe and Asia. It is the biggest city in Turkey and fills in as the nation's financial, social, and authentic center point. With its rich legacy, shocking design, clamoring markets, and various populace, Istanbul offers an exceptional mix of old customs and present day charm.

Arranged on the Bosphorus Waterway, Istanbul is separated into two unmistakable parts: the European side and the Asian side. The city's essential area has made it a critical focus of exchange, trade, and social trade over the entire course of time. It has been the capital of three significant realms, including the Roman, Byzantine, and Ottoman, which has molded its personality and left an enduring effect on its engineering wonders.

Perhaps of the most famous milestone in Istanbul is the Hagia Sophia. Initially worked as a house of God in the sixth 100 years, it later filled in as a mosque and is presently an exhibition hall. Its stupendous vault, unpredictable mosaics, and rich history make it a must-visit fascination for travelers. Another striking site is the Blue Mosque, authoritatively known as the Ruler Ahmed Mosque, famous for its dazzling blue tilework and noteworthy engineering.

The city is similarly home to the Topkapi Palace, a brilliant complex that was the super residing spot of the Ottoman rulers for very nearly four centuries. Today, it houses an exhibition that highlights Ottoman relics, including diamonds, weapons, and unique duplicates. The meandering aimlessly Impressive Market, with its tangled streets and vast shops, is a paradise for shopaholics, offering a wide display of product going from standard covers and flavors to introduce day dress and diamonds.

Istanbul's social assortment is reflected in its areas, each with its specific individual. Beyoglu is an overflowing area known for its vivacious nightlife, up-to-date bistros, and workmanship displays. Sultanahmet, the imperative heart of the city, is home to huge quantities of Istanbul's critical attractions, while Kadikoy on the Asian side emanates a really nice, bohemian climate.

The culinary scene in Istanbul is a gastronomic delight, blending flavors from various regions of Turkey and the Middle East. From sizzling kebabs and mezes to luscious Turkish deals with like baklava and Turkish delight, the city offers a feasting experience for the resources.

Furthermore, Istanbul has different broad turns of events and festivities after some time, showing its prospering articulations and music scene. The Istanbul Biennial, Istanbul Live show, and Overall Istanbul Film

Festivity are two or three examples of the city's dynamic social timetable.

Transportation in Istanbul is progressed, with an association of streetcars, transports, ships, and a state of the art metro structure communicating different bits of the city. The infamous Bosphorus Framework and the as of late evolved Eurasia Section work with development between the European and Asian sides.

In once-over, Istanbul is an enchanting city that perfectly blends its rich history in with advancement. Its stunning designing, vigorous business areas, different regions, and warm kind disposition make it an enchanting objective that entrances the hearts of visitors from around the world.

Istanbul's Top Attractions

Istanbul, the energetic city riding two expanses of land, is a city spilling over with history, culture, and building considers. As Turkey's greatest city, Istanbul offers a jackpot of attractions that will stun any visitor. The following are a part of the top attractions that make Istanbul a must-visit objective:

Hagia Sophia: An UNESCO World Heritage Site, Hagia Sophia is a plan show-stopper that has seen the climb and fall of domains. At first filled in as a Byzantine basilica, it later transformed into a mosque and is at present a display lobby. The spectacular vault, erratic mosaics, and stunning plan make it a truly hair-raising sight.

Blue Mosque (Ruler Ahmed Mosque): Another infamous picture of Istanbul, the Blue Mosque is known for its six rising above minarets and extraordinary blue tiles embellishing within walls. The mosque is at this point a working spot of affection, and visitors can experience the peacefulness and gloriousness of this holy space.

Topkapi Palace: When the home of Ottoman rulers, Topkapi Regal home offers a short investigate the excess and significance of the Ottoman Domain. Explore its astounding decks, extravagant rooms, and the Variety of escorts, where the ruler's mates and concubines lived.

Extraordinary Commercial center: Quite possibly of the most prepared and greatest covered market on earth, the Phenomenal Market is a client's paradise. With more than 4,000 shops, you can find everything from standard materials and enhancements to flavors and Turkish delights. Soak yourself in the clamoring air and arrangement for unique knickknacks.

Zing Commercial center (Egyptian Market): Arranged near the Galata Framework, the Flavor Market is a fragrant and splendid market where you can find different shocking flavors, dried natural items, nuts, and Turkish euphoria. The smell and fiery features make it a substantial joy.

Bosphorus Journey: Take a relaxing excursion along the Bosphorus Stream, which parts Istanbul among Europe and Asia. Value the city's amazing skyline, undeniable places of interest, and wonderful waterfront manors (yali). Sunset voyages are particularly supernatural, offering astounding viewpoints on the city washed in splendid light.

Basilica Capacity: Hid under the streets of Istanbul lies the Basilica Stockpiling, an old underground water store worked during the Byzantine time span. Walk around its faintly lit pathways and miracle about the lines of rising above segments and the notable Medusa heads.

Istanbul Archeological Presentation lobbies: History fans shouldn't miss the Istanbul Archeological Verifiable focuses, which house an essential combination of trinkets from various civic establishments, including the Greeks, Romans, and Ottomans. The verifiable focus complex involves the Archeological Display, the Show corridor of the Old-fashioned Arrange, and the Tiled Stand Exhibition.

Dolmabahce Imperial home: Arranged along the Bosphorus, Dolmabahce Palace is a stunning outline of Ottoman plan and extravagance. Wonder about the rich internal parts, jewel roof apparatuses, and huge nurseries. The illustrious home was the administrative focal point of the Ottoman Domain during the late nineteenth and mid 20th many years.

Istiklal Street: A clamoring bystander street in the center of Istanbul, Istiklal Street offers a mix of shopping, eating, and redirection. Stroll around the vivacious street, fixed with imperative designs, shops, bistros, and street performers. The nostalgic red trolley adds to the allure of this vigorous path.

These are two or three the various attractions that Istanbul offers of real value. The city's rich history, different culture, and enchanting blend of East and West make it a truly enamoring objective for pioneers from around the world.

Precious stones of Istanbul

Istanbul, recently known as Byzantium and Constantinople, is a city soaked with history and is home to different irrefutable objections that give declaration in regards to its rich past. From old Roman milestones to Byzantine churches and Ottoman palaces, Istanbul is a jackpot for history fans. Could we examine a piece of the striking obvious locations that magnificence the city's scene.

Hagia Sophia: At first functioned as a Byzantine church in the 6th hundred years, Hagia Sophia later filled in as a regal mosque during the Ottoman time and is right now a show lobby. This compositional gem grandstands a mix of Byzantine and Ottoman effects, with its massive vault, diverse mosaics, and stunning inside plan.

Topkapi Palace: As the super residing spot of the Ottoman rulers for just about four centuries, Topkapi Regal home remaining parts as a picture of the brilliance and luxury of the Ottoman Space. Visitors can examine the illustrious home's porches, storehouse, assortment of escorts, and different presentation entryways, pondering its stunning designing and rich credible knick-knacks.

Blue Mosque (Ruler Ahmed Mosque): This outstanding mosque, well known for its striking blue-tiled inside, was underlying the mid seventeenth 100 years. With its six minarets and streaming vaults, the Blue Mosque is an obvious achievement in Istanbul. Visitors can spectator the wonderful inside embellished with confusing calligraphy and faultless tilework.

Basilica Capacity: Known as the "Discouraged Palace," the Basilica Stockpiling is an old underground store worked in the 6th hundred years during the Byzantine time period. This colossal underground plan contains different areas, including the famous Medusa heads, which support the vaulted rooftop. Examining the supply's frightening energy is a wonderful experience.

The Spectacular Commercial center: While not rigidly an irrefutable site, the Fabulous Commercial center holds immense social significance and has a bunch of encounters following as far as possible back to the fifteenth hundred years. It is one of the world's most prepared and greatest covered markets, where visitors can soak themselves in a vivacious air while researching vast shops offering standard Turkish claims to fame, materials, flavors, and that is only the start.

The Hippodrome of Constantinople: Arranged near the Ruler Ahmed Mosque, the Hippodrome was once a focal point of chariot running and public parties during the Byzantine Space. Notwithstanding the way that its novel development has commonly vanished, visitors can regardless notification extras like the Egyptian Stone monument, Snake Segment, and Walled Support point.

The Chora Church: Generally called the Assembly of the Consecrated Hero in Chora, this Byzantine gem is applauded for its stunning mosaics and frescoes depicting scriptural scenes. Yet the gathering was changed over into a mosque during the Ottoman time span, it has been restored and saved as a presentation lobby, offering visitors a short investigate the versatile inventiveness of Byzantine times.

The Istanbul Ancient investigations Displays: Containing three separate presentation lobbies, the Istanbul Obsolete investigation Verifiable focuses house a wide grouping of relics crossing different urban foundations. Here, visitors can research shows featuring old Greek, Roman, and Byzantine antiquated rarities, including the stone final resting place of Alexander the Exceptional and the Plan of Kadesh, among others.

These are two or three cases of the irrefutable districts that make Istanbul a captivating goal. The city's layered history and different social heritage have made an extremely durable engraving on its underlying scene, making it a striking spot to research and lower oneself in history

Istanbul's Authentic focuses and Displays

Istanbul, the dynamic and significant city that rides Europe and Asia, is home to a rich social heritage. It gloats an alternate show verifiable focuses and shows that offer visitors an exceptional opportunity to jump into

52

the city's charming history, workmanship, and culture. From old relics to contemporary works of art, Istanbul's show lobbies and shows give a stunning trip through time and creative mind. The following are a couple of extraordinary establishments worth researching:

Istanbul Obsolete investigation Show lobbies: Arranged in the Sultanahmet district, the Istanbul Antiquarianism Exhibitions contain three separate designs: the Archeological Verifiable focus, the Display of the Old Orchestrate, and the Tiled Stand Authentic focus. These exhibitions house an expansive grouping of archeological doodads, including old Greek, Roman, and Ottoman relics. The highlights consolidate the Alexander Stone casket, the Game plan of Kadesh, and the Ishtar Entryway parts from Babylon.

Hagia Sophia Display: At first a Byzantine church, later different over into an Ottoman mosque, and by and by a show lobby, Hagia Sophia is a plan wonder. This UNESCO World Heritage site includes a spellbinding blend of Byzantine and Islamic parts. Inside, visitors can see the value in stunning mosaics, marvelous frescoes, and the shocking vault that has been an inspiration for quite a while.

Istanbul, the energetic and socially rich city that rides two mainlands, is a genuine heaven for food sweethearts. The feasting scene in Istanbul offers a brilliant combination of flavors impacted by Ottoman, Turkish, Center Eastern, and Mediterranean cooking styles. From road food slows down to upscale eateries, Istanbul takes special care of all palates and spending plans, offering a remarkable culinary encounter. Here is a brief look into the feasting and food scene in Istanbul.

Turkish Food: Istanbul is eminent for its true Turkish food, which is an agreeable mix of flavors, flavors, and cooking strategies. Try not to pass up on the valuable chance to attempt signature dishes like kebabs, mezes (canapés), pide (Turkish pizza), and lahmacun (Turkish flatbread finished off with minced meat and vegetables). Enjoy heavenly customary treats like baklava, Turkish joy, and sutlac (rice pudding).

Road Food: Istanbul is a paradise for road food lovers. You'll find various road merchants and food slows down selling delicious treats. Get a simit, a sesame-covered roundabout bread ring, as you investigate the city. Attempt the well known road food dish called balik ekmek, a barbecued fish sandwich, along the shores of the Bosphorus. Try not to botch the opportunity to taste kokoreç (barbecued sheep digestion tracts) or midye dolma (stuffed mussels) while meandering through the city roads.

Fish and Fish: Istanbul's essential area on the Bosphorus and its nearness to the Ocean of Marmara make it a fish darling's heaven. Along the waterfront areas, for example, Kumkapi and Arnavutkoy, you'll track down a wide exhibit of fish cafés. Devour newly got fish, barbecued or broiled, joined by mezes and a glass of raki, the conventional Turkish cocktail.

Ottoman Food: Istanbul was once the capital of the powerful Ottoman Realm, the city actually bears the impacts of its supreme past. A few eateries in Istanbul have some expertise in Ottoman cooking, offering a sample of the verifiable illustrious banquets. Attempt dishes like sheep stews, pilaf varieties, and unique Ottoman-style kebabs, which are wealthy in flavors and mirror the magnificence of the realm's culinary legacy.

Roof Eateries: Istanbul's horizon specked with minarets, vaults, and staggering perspectives on the Bosphorus gives a charming scenery to roof feasting encounters. Various cafés offer housetop porches where you can appreciate your feast while getting a charge out of all encompassing vistas of the city. These foundations frequently serve a scope of cooking styles, including Turkish and global dishes.

Current and Combination Food: Istanbul's culinary scene isn't restricted to conventional Turkish charge. The city brags a developing number current and combination cafés that mix Turkish flavors with worldwide impacts. These foundations frequently include inventive dishes, innovative introductions, and interesting mixes of fixings. They give a contemporary bend to customary Turkish food, interesting to the two local people and global guests.

Turkish Tea and Espresso Culture:

No visit to Istanbul would be finished without encountering the Turkish tea and espresso culture. Turkish tea, served in little tulip-molded glasses, is an essential piece of day to day existence in Istanbul. You'll find tea houses, known as çay bahçesi, dispersed all through the city, offering a comfortable feeling to partake in some tea. Furthermore, enjoy Turkish espresso, a solid and sweet-smelling refreshment arranged utilizing finely ground espresso beans. Remember to attempt some salep, a hot smooth beverage enhanced with orchid root, throughout the cold weather months.

All in all, eating in Istanbul is a great excursion of flavors and fragrances. Whether you're investigating the road food scene, enjoying customary Turkish dishes, or enjoying present day

Istanbul Nightlife and Amusement

Istanbul, the energetic and clamoring city spreading over the mainlands of Europe and Asia, offers a flourishing nightlife and a different scope of diversion choices. As the sun sets, the city wakes up with a variety of scenes taking care of various preferences and inclinations. From in vogue clubs to customary exhibitions, Istanbul has something for everybody to appreciate.

Clubs and Bars:

Istanbul is prestigious for its dynamic club scene, drawing in the two local people and guests from around the world. The city brags a plenty in vogue clubs where you can move the night away to an assortment of music types, including electronic, hip-bounce, and Turkish pop. Many clubs are situated in the dynamic regions of Beyoğlu, Ortaköy, and Kadıköy, offering slick insides, live DJ exhibitions, and vivacious environments. A few well known settings incorporate Reina, Fight, and Babylon.

For a more loosened up night, Istanbul offers various bars and parlors where you can mingle, appreciate unrecorded music, and enjoy a large number of drinks. You can find roof bars offering all encompassing perspectives on the city, comfortable jazz clubs with close settings, or upscale wine bars exhibiting the rich Turkish wine culture. A few remarkable choices incorporate 360 Istanbul, Babylon Bomonti, and Nardis Jazz Club.

Customary Diversion:

Istanbul additionally embraces its rich social legacy, offering conventional amusement that mirrors its verifiable roots. One high priority experience is the spinning dervishes' presentation, which grandstands the old Sufi act of turning as a type of love. These hypnotizing exhibitions can be seen at settings like the Hodjapasha Social Center and Galata Mevlevi House.

For a valid taste of Turkish old stories and music, guests can go to Turkish evenings that component live exhibitions of customary music, hip twirling, and people moves. These lively shows give a brief look into the country's brilliant practices and are in many cases joined by delightful Turkish food. Well known settings for Turkish evenings incorporate Hodjapasha Social Center and Gar Music Lobby.

Bosphorus Travels:

A remarkable method for encountering Istanbul's nightlife is by taking a Bosphorus voyage. These captivating boat trips permit you to appreciate dazzling perspectives on the city horizon enlightened around evening time while cruising along the Bosphorus Waterway. A few travels offer supper, drinks, and live diversion, making it a noteworthy and heartfelt experience.

Road Food and Bistros:

Istanbul's nightlife isn't restricted to clubs and exhibitions. The city wakes up around evening time with its dynamic road food scene and clamoring bistros. You can investigate the vivacious roads of Istiklal Road, Karaköy, and Kadıköy, where you'll find a wealth of food slows down and little diners offering tasty nearby rarities like kebabs, stuffed mussels, and sweet deals with like baklava. Furthermore, Istanbul is well known for its energetic bistro culture, with numerous foundations open until quite a bit later, giving a comfortable climate to unwind, partake in some Turkish tea or espresso, and enjoy discussion.

Istanbul's nightlife and amusement scene genuinely offer something for each taste. Whether you're looking for high-energy clubbing, social encounters, or just a casual night investigating the city's energetic roads, Istanbul has everything. The city's assorted contributions guarantee that guests and local people the same can appreciate vital evenings loaded up with energy, culture, and wonderful encounters.

Roadtrips from Istanbul

Istanbul, the dynamic and notable city traversing two landmasses, is a fantastic base for investigating the different attractions and objections in its encompassing regions. In the event that you're hoping to branch out of the city for a roadtrip, here are a few energizing choices to consider:

Bursa: Found south of Istanbul, Bursa is known as the "Green City" because of its lavish stops and gardens. It's renowned for its memorable destinations, including the Great Mosque (Ulu Cami) and the Bursa Stronghold. Try not to miss a visit to the famous Bursa Silk Market and a restoring experience in the warm showers.

Sovereigns' Islands: A short ship ride from Istanbul's shores will take you to the Rulers' Islands, a gathering of nine islands in the Ocean of Marmara. These islands offer a serene departure from the clamoring city, without any vehicles permitted. Investigate the beguiling roads, lease a bike or a pony drawn carriage, and partake in the quiet sea shores.

Gallipoli Promontory: For history fans, a roadtrip to the Gallipoli Landmass is an unquestionable requirement. This critical The Second Great War combat zone is a position of recognition and highlights a few commemorations and burial grounds. Take a directed visit to find out about the verifiable occasions and offer your appreciation to the fallen fighters.

Troy: Leave on an excursion to the old city of Troy, situated close to the Dardanelles. This UNESCO World Legacy Site is saturated with folklore and archeological marvels. Investigate the remnants, stroll through the reproduced antiquated city walls, and see the popular wooden pony.

Edirne: Known as the second capital of the Ottoman Realm, Edirne is a city wealthy in engineering wonders. Its highlight is the Selimiye Mosque, a show-stopper of Ottoman engineering. Visit the memorable locales like the Edirne Royal residence and the Old Mosque, and drench yourself in the city's dynamic marketplaces.

Sapanca: Settled in the midst of beautiful scenes and a tranquil lake, Sapanca offers a quiet retreat from the city. Partake in the lovely landscape, take a relaxed stroll along the lake, or enjoy water sports like kayaking or paddleboarding. Sapanca is additionally renowned for its nearby food, so don't botch the opportunity to attempt a few heavenly provincial dishes.

Yalova: Situated on the southern shoreline of the Ocean of Marmara, Yalova is known for its warm springs and regular excellence. Loosen up in the mending waters of the warm spas, leave in the close by forested regions, or visit the beautiful Karaca Arboretum to observe the assorted vegetation.

These are only a couple of the numerous roadtrip choices from Istanbul. Whether you're keen on history, nature, or just investigating enchanting towns, there is something for everybody reachable for this captivating city

Cappadocia Outline

Cappadocia is an enamoring locale situated in focal Anatolia, Turkey. Known for its exceptional land developments, old history, and rich social legacy, Cappadocia has turned into a famous vacationer location and an UNESCO World Legacy site. Its stunning scenes, comprising of pixie stacks, cave residences, and extensive valleys, make it a genuinely exceptional spot to visit.

Topographically, Cappadocia is described by its volcanic developments. A long period of time back, volcanic emissions covered the district with a thick layer of debris, which at last cemented into delicate stone known as tuff. After some time, wind and water disintegration shaped this stone into a strange scene of transcending cone-molded rock developments, frequently alluded to as pixie chimney stacks. These exceptional designs are one of the characterizing highlights of Cappadocia and draw in guests from everywhere the world.

The verifiable meaning of Cappadocia goes back millennia. The area has been possessed since ancient times and has been home to different civic establishments, including the Hittites, Persians, Greeks, Romans, Byzantines, and Ottomans. Its essential area along old shipping lanes added to its social variety and affected the engineering, workmanship, and customs tracked down nearby.

One of the most striking parts of Cappadocia is its underground urban communities. Underneath the surface, a tremendous organization of passages and chambers was cut out of the delicate stone by early Christian people group looking for shelter from oppression. These underground urban communities, like Derinkuyu and Kaymakli, gave haven, stockpiling, and places of love. Today, guests can investigate these intriguing underground edifices and gain knowledge into the existences of individuals who once lived there.

Cappadocia's rich history is likewise reflected in its various stone cut chapels and cloisters. Finished with perplexing frescoes tracing all the way back to the Byzantine time, these strict locales offer a brief look into the district's Christian legacy. The Göreme Outdoors Gallery is an especially famous objective, highlighting a few stone cut chapels embellished with shocking scriptural scenes and strict symbols.

Notwithstanding its geographical and authentic marvels, Cappadocia is famous for its tourist balloon rides. The locale's dreamlike scenes give the ideal setting to an otherworldly inflatable flight, offering stunning all encompassing perspectives on the pixie stacks, valleys, and towns underneath. The experience of floating above Cappadocia at the crack of dawn or nightfall has turned into a notorious and profoundly sought-after action for guests.

Besides, Cappadocia offers different open air exercises for nature lovers and experience searchers. The locale flaunts various climbing trails that breeze through its valleys, permitting guests to investigate the beautiful scenes by walking. Guests can likewise appreciate horseback riding, quad trekking, and even stay in cave lodgings or shop facilities cut into the stone developments.

In synopsis, Cappadocia is a really phenomenal objective that offers a novel mix of regular miracles, verifiable importance, and social legacy. Its strange scenes, underground urban communities, rock-cut chapels, and exciting sight-seeing balloon rides make it a must-visit area for voyagers looking for a remarkable encounter. Cappadocia proceeds to dazzle and motivate guests with its supernatural appeal and ageless magnificence.

Pixie Chimney stacks and Scenes

Pixie chimney stacks and exceptional scenes are enrapturing regular developments that grandstand the marvels of our planet's topography and the different powers that shape it. These unprecedented highlights can be tracked down in different areas all over the planet and have long caught the creative mind of the two local people and explorers the same.

Pixie smokestacks are especially common in the district of Cappadocia, situated in focal Turkey. These topographical arrangements are the aftereffect of millennia of volcanic action, disintegration, and enduring. They are portrayed by tall, cone-molded rock arrangements that look like stacks, with eccentric and extraordinary appearances. The name "pixie smokestacks" is gotten from neighborhood legends, which recommends that these designs were once possessed by enchanted creatures.

The development cycle of pixie fireplaces starts with antiquated volcanic ejections that saved layers of debris, magma, and basalt in the district. Over the long haul, wind and water disintegration shaped the delicate stone layers, making the extraordinary cone-like designs. The harder top layers, like basalt, went about as defensive covers, forestalling further disintegration of the fundamental milder stone. This brought about the particular mushroom-like state of the fireplaces.

Past their fascinating appearance, pixie smokestacks play had a huge impact in mankind's set of experiences. The old occupants of Cappadocia perceived the appropriateness of these arrangements for home and began cutting out residences, chapels, and cloisters inside them. These cavern like designs gave normal protection and insurance from the district's super weather patterns. A portion of these cavern residences, known as "pixie chimney stack houses," are as yet occupied today, while others have been changed over into lodgings, eateries, and vacation destinations.

Aside from Cappadocia, there are different spots all over the planet where extraordinary scenes charm the creative mind. The Zhangjiajie Public Backwoods Park in China is eminent for its transcending sandstone points of support, frequently covered in fog, which filled in as motivation for the drifting mountains portrayed in the film "Symbol." These dreamlike developments, otherwise called the "Thank heaven Mountains," are a consequence of quartzite sandstone disintegration north of millions of years.

One more exceptional scene can be found in the Salar de Uyuni, the world's biggest salt level, situated in Bolivia. This huge breadth of blindingly white salt outside layer extends as may be obvious, making a dreamlike and apparently perpetual skyline. During the blustery season, a flimsy layer of water covers the salt level, changing it into a monster reflect that mirrors the sky above. This normal peculiarity makes hypnotizing optical deceptions and draws in picture takers and swashbucklers from around the world.

Novel scenes like pixie fireplaces, sandstone points of support, and salt pads are a demonstration of the sensational excellence and variety of our planet. They help us to remember the strong geographical powers that have formed and keep on molding the Earth, abandoning striking sights that mix our minds. Investigating these unprecedented developments permits us to see the value in the marvels of nature and gain a more profound comprehension of our reality's rich history and geographical legacy.

Cappadocia Inflatable Experience

tourist balloon rides in Cappadocia

A Mystical Encounter

Cappadocia, situated in focal Turkey, is eminent for its stunning scenes, special stone developments, and antiquated cave abodes. One of the most well known and charming ways of investigating this enrapturing district is through a tourist balloon ride. Offering a higher perspective of the dreamlike scene, a sight-seeing balloon ride in Cappadocia is an extraordinary encounter that will leave you in stunningness.

As the sun ascends into the great beyond, painting the sky with lively shades of orange and pink, many sight-seeing balloons begin to blow up in the pre-day break light. The actual sight is an exhibition to observe. When the inflatables are prepared, you move on board the wicker bin, and with a delicate arrival of hot air, the inflatable begins to rise, conveying you high up.

As you float higher, the pixie stacks, transcending rock developments that look like something out of a dream story, materialize. These novel topographical arrangements were made north of millions of years through the disintegration of volcanic debris and tuff. The delicate morning light gives occasion to feel qualms about an otherworldly shine these designs, emphasizing their multifaceted subtleties and fluctuated shapes. Maybe you're floating through a fanciful world suspended in time.

The scene of Cappadocia is specked with old cavern residences, cloisters, and houses of worship cut into the delicate stone. From a higher place, you can see the complicated organization of passages and chambers, uncovering the rich history of the district. The gifted pilots move the inflatables with accuracy, taking you near these memorable locales, permitting you to wonder about the design marvels of the past.

The perspectives from the sight-seeing balloon are just stunning. The immense scope of the Cappadocian valleys loosens up underneath you, with moving slopes, grape plantations, and plantations making an interwoven of varieties and surfaces. The serenity of the experience is just broken by a periodic sound of the burner as the pilot changes the height, offering you an alternate point of view of this staggering scene.

The whole sight-seeing balloon ride goes on about 60 minutes, albeit the recollections will endure forever. As the flight reaches a conclusion, you drop tenderly back to the ground, where a champagne toast anticipates to commend your remarkable experience. The team assists you with securely landing from the bushel, and you can think about the remarkable sights you saw from a higher place.

Cappadocia's tourist balloon rides have become tremendously famous, drawing guests from all sides of the globe. It's prudent to book your ride ahead of time, particularly during the pinnacle vacationer season, to get your spot in this mystical experience. While the weather patterns assume a critical part in deciding if the inflatables can take off, Cappadocia is known for its positive flying circumstances, making it a solid objective for blistering air expanding.

Whether you're a daredevil, a nature darling, or a set of experiences fan, a sight-seeing balloon ride in Cappadocia Quite possibly of the most renowned underground city in Cappadocia is Derinkuyu. A broad complex expands roughly 85 meters (279 feet) underneath the surface and flaunts various levels, interconnected burrows, ventilation shafts, wells, and, surprisingly, a sanctuary. Derinkuyu, with its great ability to house huge number of individuals, filled in as a safe space during seasons of intrusion and given security against different dangers, including strikes by adjoining civilizations and oppressions from the beginning of time.

One more remarkable underground city in Cappadocia is Kaymakli. Comparable in plan and reason to Derinkuyu, Kaymakli offers a captivating look into the underground existence of old Cappadocians. With its unmistakable highlights, for example, pens, extra spaces, kitchens, and wineries, Kaymakli exhibits the independence and complex social design that existed inside these underground networks.

Past the underground urban areas, Cappadocia is likewise famous for its cavern homes. The locale's special geographical arrangements, known as "pixie stacks," comprise of volcanic debris and basalt that dissolved north of millions of years, bringing about transcending cone-like designs. These pixie stacks gave a characteristic material to individuals of Cappadocia to cut out cave homes.

The cavern residences of Cappadocia were not just crude habitations; they were many-sided multi-story homes, frequently interconnected with underground ways and passages. These caverns offered security from the cruel Anatolian environment, giving a cool shelter in singing summers and protection against cold winters. Some cavern homes were even beautified with frescoes, displaying the imaginative abilities of their occupants.

Cappadocia's underground urban communities and buckle residences play had an imperative impact in protecting the district's set of experiences and social legacy. Today, large numbers of these designs have been perceived as UNESCO World Legacy Locales, drawing in vacationers from around the globe who are anxious to investigate their secret profundities and experience the exceptional combination of nature and human craftsmanship.

Visiting Cappadocia permits you to meander through the complex passages, wonder about the designing accomplishments of the old occupants, and gain a more profound comprehension of the strength and versatility of human progress. Whether investigating the tremendous underground urban communities or wandering into the unpredictably cut cave homes, Cappadocia offers a really remarkable excursion into the profundities of history.

Cappadocia's Underground Ponders

Underground Urban communities and Cavern Abodes in Cappadocia

Cappadocia, a verifiable district situated in focal Anatolia, Turkey, is famous for its one of a kind underground urban communities and cavern residences. These exceptional designs date back millennia and have dazzled guests with their engineering inventiveness and verifiable importance. We should dive into the captivating universe of underground urban communities and cavern homes in Cappadocia.

Cappadocia's underground urban communities are a demonstration of the cleverness and versatility of its old occupants. These underground edifices were basically cut out of delicate volcanic stone known as tuff, which is plentiful in the district. Individuals of Cappadocia started making these underground urban areas as soon as the Hittite period, around the fourteenth century BCE, and kept extending and changing them throughout the long term.

Perhaps of the most well known underground city in Cappadocia is Derinkuyu. A broad complex expands roughly 85 meters (279 feet) underneath the surface and flaunts various levels, interconnected burrows, ventilation shafts, wells, and, surprisingly, a house of prayer. Derinkuyu, with its great ability to house huge number of individuals, filled in as a safe space during seasons of intrusion and given security against different dangers, including strikes by adjoining civic establishments and mistreatments since the beginning of time.

One more striking underground city in Cappadocia is Kaymakli. Comparative in plan and reason to Derinkuyu, Kaymakli offers a captivating look into the underground existence of old Cappadocians. With its unmistakable elements, for example, corrals, extra spaces, kitchens, and wineries, Kaymakli exhibits the independence and complex social design that existed inside these underground networks.

Past the underground urban areas, Cappadocia is likewise prestigious for its cavern homes. The locale's extraordinary geographical developments, known as "pixie chimney stacks," comprise of volcanic debris and basalt that disintegrated more than great many years, bringing about transcending cone-like designs. These pixie smokestacks gave a characteristic material to individuals of Cappadocia to cut out cave homes.

The cavern homes of Cappadocia were not simply crude habitations; they were complex multi-story residences, frequently interconnected with underground ways and passages. These caverns offered security from the cruel Anatolian environment, giving a cool shelter in searing summers and protection against cold winters. Some cavern residences were even enhanced with frescoes, displaying the creative gifts of their occupants.

Cappadocia's underground urban communities and buckle homes play had a fundamental impact in protecting the locale's set of experiences and social legacy. Today, a considerable lot of these designs have been perceived as UNESCO World Legacy Destinations, drawing in vacationers from around the globe who are anxious to investigate their secret profundities and experience the wonderful combination of nature and human craftsmanship.

Visiting Cappadocia permits you to meander through the confounded passages, wonder about the designing accomplishments of the old occupants, and gain a more profound comprehension of the flexibility and versatility of human civilization. Whether investigating the huge underground urban communities or wandering into the unpredictably cut cave residences, Cappadocia offers a genuinely unprecedented excursion into the profundities of history.

Climbing and Outside Exercises in Cappadocia

Cappadocia, with its one of a kind topographical developments and shocking regular scenes, offers an abundance of chances for climbing and outside exercises. Whether you're a devoted explorer, a courageous soul, or just somebody who appreciates being encircled by stunning landscape, Cappadocia is a heaven ready to be investigated. How about we plunge into the assorted scope of open air exercises and climbing trails that look for you in this enthralling area.

Climbing in Cappadocia: Cappadocia's strange scenes give an extraordinary scenery to climbing fans. The valleys, pixie fireplaces, and old stone developments make a beautiful setting for open air investigation. A portion of the famous climbing trails incorporate the Rose Valley, Love Valley, Pigeon Valley, and Red Valley. Each trail offers its own remarkable appeal, from transcending rock arrangements to stowed away cavern holy places decorated with frescoes. En route, you'll experience staggering perspectives, intriguing stone arrangements, and old cavern homes, giving an extraordinary climbing experience.

Sight-seeing Balloon Rides: A tourist balloon ride is a must-do movement in Cappadocia, offering an elevated perspective of the district's stunning scenes. As the sun rises, brilliant sight-seeing balloons fill the sky, making an otherworldly scene. Floating over the pixie fireplaces, valleys, and grape plantations, you'll observer the strange excellence of Cappadocia according to a special viewpoint.

Horseback Riding: Investigating Cappadocia riding a horse is a phenomenal method for drenching yourself in the locale's regular miracles. Horseback riding visits take you through the valleys, grape plantations, and old pathways, permitting you to partake in the serenity of the scene while holding with these glorious creatures. Experienced guides lead the way, guaranteeing a protected and noteworthy experience.

Cycling: Cappadocia's different territory and organization of trails make it a phenomenal objective for cycling devotees. Whether you incline toward relaxed rides through the valleys or testing mountain trekking trails, Cappadocia offers choices for all expertise levels. Lease a bicycle, follow the very much checked trails, and pedal your direction through the remarkable scenes, finding unlikely treasures en route.

Jeep Safaris: For those looking for an undeniably exhilarating rough terrain experience, Jeep safaris are a famous decision. Jump on board a 4x4 vehicle and investigate the tough territories, outside of what might be expected paths, and far off towns of Cappadocia. With an accomplished driver in the driver's seat, you'll navigate through valleys, cross rough scenes, and witness all encompassing vistas that will leave you in wonder.

Rock Climbing: Cappadocia's interesting stone developments make it a safe house for rock climbing devotees. The district offers an assortment of climbing courses reasonable for the two fledglings and experienced climbers. Take part in this elating action as you scale the upward walls and bluffs, partaking in the staggering perspectives from the top.

Setting up camp: Going through a night under the brilliant Cappadocian sky is an extraordinary encounter. There are assigned setting up camp regions where you can set up your tent and partake in the serenity of the environmental factors. As dimness falls, you'll observer the hypnotizing sight of innumerable stars enlightening the night sky, making a mysterious feeling.

Whether you decide to climb through the captivating valleys, take off over the scenes in a sight-seeing balloon, leave on an adrenaline-siphoning experience, or essentially drench yourself in the peacefulness of nature, Cappadocia offers many open air exercises to suit each taste and inclination. In this way, put on your climbing boots, get your camera, and prepare for a remarkable excursion into the normal marvels of Cappadocia.

Cappadocia Food and Wine.

Nearby Cooking and Wine sampling in Cappadocia

Cappadocia, situated in the core of Turkey, isn't just known for its shocking scenes and antiquated rock developments yet additionally for its rich culinary customs and outstanding neighborhood cooking. This district offers a novel gastronomic encounter, where you can enjoy scrumptious dishes.